ONLY MYSTERY

Solo el misterio
nos hace vivir
Solo el misterio

University Press of Florida
Gainesville
Tallahassee
Tampa
Boca Raton
Pensacola
Orlando
Miami
Jacksonville

ONLY

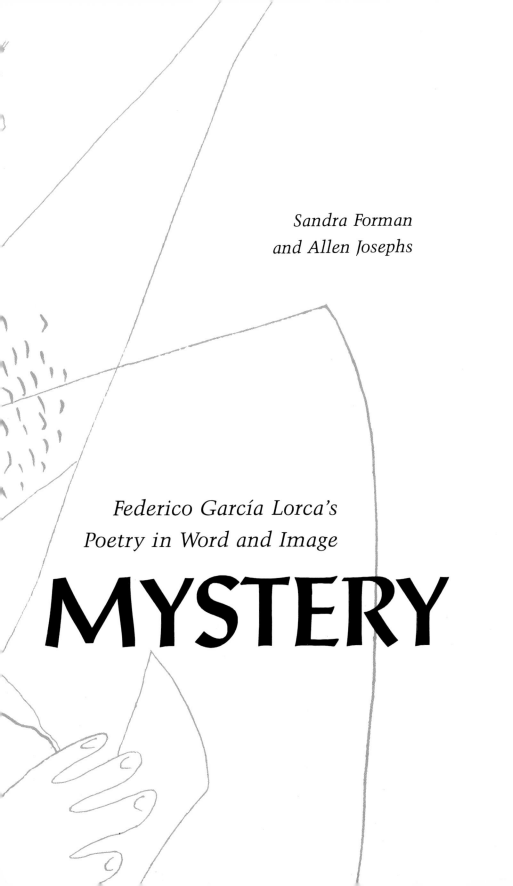

*Sandra Forman
and Allen Josephs*

*Federico García Lorca's
Poetry in Word and Image*

MYSTERY

Publication of this volume was made possible in part by the
Program for Cultural Cooperation between Spain's Ministry of
culture and United States' Universities.

Copyright 1992 by the Board of Regents of the
State of Florida
Printed in Hong Kong on acid-free paper
All rights reserved

96 95 94 93 92 5 4 3 2 1

Library of Congress Cataloging in Publication Data

García Lorca, Federico, 1898–1936.
Only Mystery: Federico García Lorca's poetry in
word and image / Sandra Forman and Allen
Josephs.
p. cm.
Includes bibliographical references and index.
ISBN 0-8130-1133-7
I. Forman, Sandra H.   II. Josephs, Allen.
III. Title.
PQ6613.A763A6   1992   92-1285
861'.62—dc20   CIP

Spanish texts by Federico García Lorca from *Obras
completas* copyright 1986, 1992 by Herederos de
Federico García Lorca. Drawings by Federico
García Lorca copyright 1992 by Fundacion Federico
García Lorca. Used with permission. All rights
reserved.

Translations of Spanish texts by Federico García
Lorca copyright 1992 by Allen Josephs and
Herederos de Federico García Lorca.

The University Press of Florida is the scholarly
publishing agency of the State University System
of Florida, comprised of Florida A & M University,
Florida Atlantic University, Florida International
University, Florida State University, University of
Central Florida, University of Florida, University
of North Florida, University of South Florida, and
University of West Florida.

University Press of Florida
15 Northwest 15th Street
Gainesville, FL 32611

For Willis Edward Hopper *in memoriam,*
Dorothy Hendrix Josephs *in memoriam,*
and Rick Holmberg, M.D.

CONTENTS

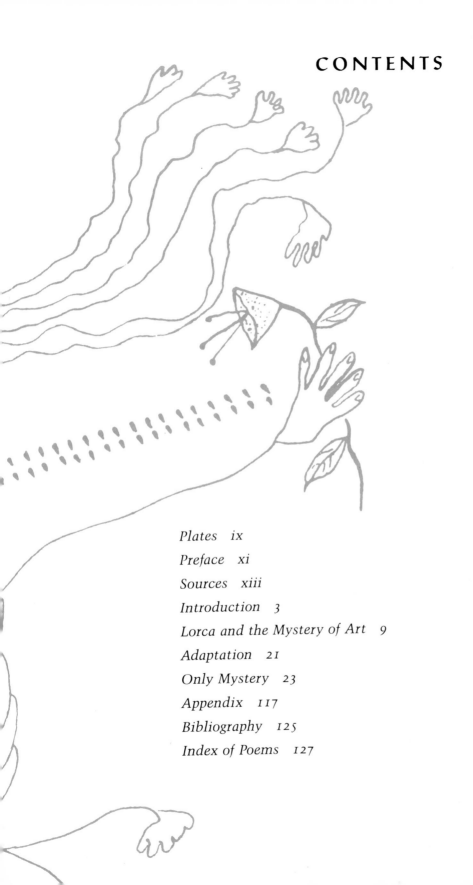

PLATES

PREFACE

IN HIS STUDY of the new physics Gary Zukav points out that "the profound physicists of this century increasingly have become aware that they are confronting the ineffable." He cites Max Planck, the father of quantum mechanics: "Science . . . means unresting endeavor and continually progressing development toward an aim which the poetic intuition may apprehend, but which the intellect can never fully grasp" (313). *Which poetic intuition may apprehend. . . .* Planck's statement about science with its reliance on intuition over intellect bears a remarkable resemblance to what Federico García Lorca once said about the nature of poetic mystery: "Through poetry man more quickly approaches the edge where the philosopher and the mathematician turn their backs in silence" (III, 343).

This book is intended for all readers who choose to approach that edge, who seek expression of the ineffable, who somehow know intuitively, as Lorca did, that behind the dense veil of mystery, all things exist "in a tender intimacy, volcanoes, ants, zephyrs and the great night hugging itself about the waist with the Milky Way" (III, 318).

Many people helped realize the original staged production of *Only Mystery: Lorca's Poetry in Performance*. The list of program acknowledgments was extensive, and we herein reiterate our heartfelt gratitude to those people in North Carolina and Florida.

The transition from those stages to these pages as *Only Mystery: Federico García Lorca's Poetry in Word and Image* was made possible through the faith, encouragement, and support of Professor Emerita Margaret Sayers Peden, University of Missouri; Provost Douglas D. Friedrich and President Morris L. Marx, University of West Florida, Pensacola; Manuel Fernández-Montesinos García and the Fundación Federico García Lorca, Madrid; Larry Leshan, layout artist, and Judy Goffman, editor, University Press of Florida.

SOURCES

THE MOST READILY available and convenient source for Lorca's work in the original is the *Obras completas* published by Aguilar in Madrid. We have used the latest three-volume edition of 1986, indicating volume number and page number after each poem or prose section. With the exception of one phrase from Philip Cummings cited in the Epilogue (a phrase which is not known to exist in Spanish), all translations are by Allen Josephs. In the introductory materials and in the script we have cited other authors or editors by name and page number, giving complete references in the Bibliography.

As of 1990, there exists a catalogue raisonné of Lorca's graphic art. Coordinated by Manuel Fernández-Montesinos of the Fundación Federico García Lorca and compiled and written by Mario Hernández, *Libro de los dibujos de Federico García Lorca* is the definitive reference work for Lorca's drawings. In the List of Plates we have included in brackets the corresponding catalogue number for each of the drawings herein reproduced (see Bibliography for complete reference, including English translation).

The introductory essay, "Lorca and the Mystery of Art," by Allen Josephs, is a distillation and adaptation of previous essays, drawing in particular from *White Wall of Spain: The Mysteries of Andalusian Culture*, the title of which derives from Lorca's verse: ¡Oh blanco muro de España! Oh, white wall of Spain! (I, 555).

ONLY MYSTERY

Federico García Lorca, Granada, 1919. Photo by Rogelio Robles Romero Saavedra. Courtesy of Fundación Federico García Lorca.

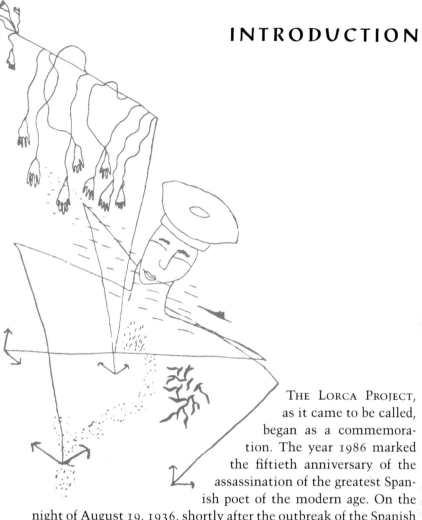

INTRODUCTION

THE LORCA PROJECT, as it came to be called, began as a commemoration. The year 1986 marked the fiftieth anniversary of the assassination of the greatest Spanish poet of the modern age. On the night of August 19, 1936, shortly after the outbreak of the Spanish civil war, Federico García Lorca was senselessly executed by a death squad and his body dumped into a common grave outside his native city of Granada. We chose the passage of half a century since that tragic moment to commemorate Lorca's life and his works by organizing a symposium called "Lorca: His Poetry and Theatre in Theory and Practice."

During Generalísimo Francisco Franco's forty-year rule, Lorca's work suffered a kind of tacit eclipse in Spain since his death was seen, at best, as a tragic blunder of the regime. With the advent of Spanish democracy, however, Lorca's memory rapidly achieved legendary status as a fitting and poetic symbol for liberty. His poetry and theatre quickly attained the pre-eminence they had deserved, while abroad Lorca became the most widely translated Spanish writer of all time.

By 1986, the fiftieth anniversary of his death and of the beginning of the Spanish civil war, interest in Lorca increased, and new biographies of his life, new translations of his works, and new productions of his plays were in progress around the world. Yet in spite of such global attention, Lorca is one of the least read or understood of the truly great artists of the twentieth century in the English-speaking world. A major reason for the commemorative symposium was to present Lorca's work to those not fully acquainted with his genius.

On a rain-drenched January 16, 1987, at the University of North Carolina at Greensboro, performers and scholars from a variety of fields—theatre, oral interpretation, English, Spanish, history—joined forces to celebrate Lorca's achievements. One of the most successful parts of that memorable evening of performance and discussion was a brief, staged reading of some of Lorca's poems by student actors from the newly formed Readers Theatre Ensemble and by guest actress Isabel Garcia-Lorca, the poet's niece. The success of that early collaborative effort (new translations of the poems by Josephs, direction of the readings by Forman), increased our desire and determination to undertake a full-length Readers Theatre script based on Lorca's work.

Much of Lorca's poetry is ideally suited to the medium of Readers Theatre, which may be defined in the most general terms as the presentation of literature on the stage. His poems are filled with actual characters from Spanish life ranging from antiquity to the present—Romans, Carthaginians, Jews, saints, virgins, Gypsies, smugglers, *toreros*. "I do not conceive of poetry as an abstraction but as a real existing thing which has passed next to me," he once wrote. "All the characters in my poems have existed," he claimed with perhaps characteristic overstatement (III, 671).

Lorca's poetry is intentionally dramatic, portraying loves, seductions, rapes, murders, martyrdoms, in effect an entire series of highly dramatic scenes that present a dynamic vision of the world of Andalucía in southern Spain. But there is another side to Lorca's poetry. In 1929 and 1930, Lorca made an extended visit to New York. In the poems about his New York experience, he produced a chilling vision of the modern metropolis rising in opposition to the natural beauty of his Spanish homeland. Watching bankrupt men jumping out of windows on Wall Street, urging Harlem blacks to revolt against their oppressors, denouncing materialism from the top of the Chrysler Building, Lorca became the voice of the natural poet crying in an urban wilderness. These unnervingly prophetic poems revealed a different dimension of his poetic genius. We believed the juxtaposition of the Andalusian poems and the New York poems would have a double appeal for audiences.

Always reluctant to publish his poetry in book form, Lorca insisted that it was meant to be recited rather than read. During his life, like an ancient bard, he became famous for reciting his own work, often singing and accompanying himself on the piano. In putting together the script, we kept Lorca's dramatic flair in mind, choosing poems that were at once characteristic of his best work and yet well suited to performance on stage. He once remarked that theatre was the poetry that rose up out of the book and became human (III, 673). We took that phrase literally by taking his poetry out of the book and putting it on stage, in the process returning his poetry to the living sources from which it had evolved.

The primary idea was to compile a script that would simultaneously present Lorca's poetry and his ideas about poetry in a loosely biographical sequence, a script that, with the proper production, would transport the members of the audience to Lorca's world, acquaint them with the artist and his ideas, and make them experience and understand many of his finest poems. Fidelity to Lorca's own vision of art and life was always foremost in our minds.

The fact that Lorca is as little known as he is in the English-speaking world—or, more precisely, as little understood and appreciated outside the circles of Hispanism—has been something of a mystery in itself. It is possible to attribute some of the blame to the early translations, but it may be more accurate to point to the larger problem of cultural context. Within the confines of the twentieth century and Western tradition, it is difficult to find a great artist more radically divergent from our own cultural norms than Lorca. Of the great modernists only his fellow Andalusian, Picasso, can seem as totally *other*.

Bearing that radical *otherness* in mind, we determined to do two things: to use only our own translations (with the exception of one phrase known only in English and cited by Philip Cummings) and to preserve Lorca's unique cultural context as much as possible. We have not tried to make the poet sound like an Anglophone and have left many recognizable words or phrases in Spanish on purpose. Lorca is often rightly called the most Spanish of artists, so we did nothing to adapt or de-emphasize his cultural heritage. By using our own translations throughout, we also hoped to gain dramatic cohesiveness and unity of tone.

Rather than using a live actor on stage, we disembodied the voice of Lorca (and of the child in the first poem) by using a tape recording. The rest of the material was broken down for seven voices, which is to say seven actors, used individually and in chorus. The appropriateness of that choice, the selection and order of the poems and prose sections, and other such intricacies of collaboration, are matters we believe best left unaddressed. To explain the mystery of the creative process, it would be necessary to attempt to describe, among many other things, the effect—the inspiration—of the air and the people of Andalucía, of green mornings in June on the patio of the Garcia-Lorca house in Narixa where we worked, of early southwest breezes off *Mare Nostrum*, of *lagartos* (lizards) basking on the white wall. Instead, we prefer to let the script speak for itself.

In the production we had accompaniment by live and taped music, and to help create the unusual cultural context of Lorca's poetry, we used a variety of visuals, principally color slides of Andalucía, including specific locations appropriate to the poems. We also used selected historical photographs of Lorca, of his characters, such as *torero* Ignacio Sánchez Mejías, and of historical locations, particularly New York in 1929–30.

If Lorca's poetry is insufficiently appreciated in English, his drawings are virtually unknown. Yet they frequently parallel his poems and sometimes offer striking illustrations for them. The production relied frequently on these highly original art works, and this book, absent our actors, relies on them even more, creating on the page a sometimes unexpected synergy.

According to Helen Oppenheimer, "The visual images he created often contain the germ of an idea which he later elaborated in a sophisticated piece of writing. They are not mere decoration. They are a key to understanding the man and his literary achievements" (9). Whether we see the drawings as germs of an idea for a poem or view them as illustrations that help us see the poems in a better light is probably less important than the engaging syn-

A white-walled Andalusian *pueblo.* Photo by Allen Josephs, 1987.

esthesia produced by experiencing them together. To that end we have searched through Lorca's work for the echo of a drawing and the picture of a poem.

Joan Miró once remarked that Lorca's drawings seemed to him the work of a poet, which was, he said, the highest praise he could render any graphic expression ("Dibujos"). Lorca would surely have been pleased with the remark since in his own words the drawings were "simultaneously pure poetry or pure plastic expression" (III, 970). For him the two were virtually inseparable.

In a lecture on modern art Lorca theorized that painting had become very old and wise and that now (in 1928) it must "shed its old skin and become childlike, sister of the stylizations of cave paintings and first cousin of the exquisite art of primitive tribes" (III, 278). That deft triangulation—the kinship of modern, ancient, and primitive—is a succinct expression of Lorca's artistic

Lorca at the piano, Granada, 1935, wearing the coverall of La Barraca, the national touring theatre that he directed. Courtesy of Fundación Federico García Lorca.

ideals, an expression we believe will be everywhere evident in the pages that follow.

Actor, director, scene designer, pianist, painter, essayist, playwright, and poet, Lorca was a consummate artist with an extraordinary sense of mission and dedication to his craft. It is that overarching aesthetic sense that we kept foremost in mind in order to create not a mere anthology of his poetry but a script and a book that reflected an entire mise-en-scène in the largest sense of that term: milieu; or better yet, the Spanish word, *ambiente*; a biographical, poetic anthology in word and in image.

This introduction is both a brief history of the script we have compiled and an introduction to the book that contains the script. The mystery of theatre cannot endure, except in memory, beyond the moment of its performance. It is our hope, however, that this book preserve in English the sense of mystery that inspired Federico García Lorca, in his theatre, in his poetry, and in his art, for it was his sense of mystery that inspired us. "*Sólo el misterio nos hace vivir*," he wrote at the foot of one of his drawings. "*Sólo el misterio*." "Only mystery makes us live. Only mystery" (III, 1038).

LORCA AND
THE MYSTERY OF ART

*The following essay by Allen
Josephs provides cultural
background for Lorca's complex
world and serves as a prelude
for the script. It is the keynote
address, with minor changes,
delivered on January 16, 1987,
at the University of North
Carolina at Greensboro, to open
the symposium "Lorca: His
Poetry and Theatre in Theory
and Practice."*

FEDERICO GARCÍA LORCA is unquestionably the premier Spanish
writer of our age and perhaps of all time, having now surpassed
even Cervantes in number of translations. Although many may be
more familiar with the brilliant eccentricities of Lorca's once
close friend, Salvador Dalí, the only Spanish artist who can truly
be compared to Lorca is Picasso. Had Lorca lived to Picasso's ripe
old age, he would still be alive today and would no doubt have
produced a body of work as rich, as varied, and as monumental as
Picasso's. In spite of the fact that Lorca was cut down at the
youthful age of thirty-eight, they had much more in common
than is generally recognized.

Both were from the southern region of Spain, called Andalucía,
the site of the oldest culture in the Western world. Partly as a
result of that ancient heritage, both were radically conservative in
matters of art, yet both were brilliantly innovative as well. More
than any other modernists, Lorca and Picasso helped us understand that ancient and modern were really two sides of the same

9

Lorca, 1904. Courtesy of
Fundacion Federico García
Lorca.

coin. Finally, both the painter from Malaga and the writer from
Granada believed unswervingly in the mystery of art.

In order to arrive at what I mean by the mystery of art, I would
like to begin with the story of my introduction to Lorca. Harold
Bloom is right, I think, when he reminds us that the critic's mission is to tell us why it matters to read, and in that context I want
to explain why it mattered to me to read Lorca.

The story begins one sweltering summer day in 1963 when a
young college dropout—who dropped out in part because he had
not passed Spanish—drove with the American *matador*, John
Fulton, from Madrid to Sevilla. As they swept through the arid
rolling plains of La Mancha, past the ancient windmills Don
Quijote took to be giants, and down through the pass at
Despenaperros where the Moslems and the Christians threw each

other off the cliffs a thousand years ago and where the ancient Iberians worshipped their gods two thousand years before that, and finally into and along the long rich valley of the Guadalquivir River where European civilization began, the *matador* recited poetry to the college dropout.

I, of course, was the fugitive and the poetry was Lorca's "Lament for Ignacio Sánchez Mejías." By that time, having become an avid *aficionado* of the *corrida de toros* (what we erroneously call the bullfight), I had spent about eight months in Spain and so I could understand much of what John Fulton was reciting. In my mind's ear I can still hear his recitation:

> At five in the afternoon.
> It was exactly five in the afternoon.
>
> The rest was death and only death
> *At five in the afternoon.*
>
> Ay, that awful five in the afternoon!
> It was five on all the clocks!
> It was five in the shadow of the afternoon!

John was reciting in Spanish and the repetitious verses had an irresistible, tolling, almost magical effect, falling somewhere between litany and liturgy:

> A las cinco de la tarde.
> Eran las cinco en punto de la tarde.
>
> Lo demás era muerte y sólo muerte
> *A las cinco de la tarde.*
>
> ¡Ay qué terribles cinco de la tarde!
> ¡Eran las cinco en todos los relojes!
> ¡Eran las cinco en sombra de la tarde! (I, 551–52)

That recitation eventually led the college dropout to write a dissertation on Lorca's theatre. From the beginning, then, there was a kind of practical value in those verses. In part because of them, because their effect fascinated me, I returned to school, and *mutatis mutandis* ended up teaching and writing about Spanish literature and civilization. Those verses somehow summed up then what I felt about Spain, what I loved about Spain, and what mystified me about Spain. In no small measure they gave my life and my career direction.

When I first arrived in Spain at the age of nineteen, I understood strangely that I had somehow come home to a place I had never been before. Some months later when John Fulton introduced me to Lorca's poetry, I began a personal quest to understand the reasons behind that sense of belonging. Although my odyssey would take another twenty years to complete, I knew intuitively on that distant summer afternoon that Lorca's verses had kindled the fires of passion that until then had only smoldered in my imagination.

Reading everything Lorca wrote eventually turned into a kind of revelation, because to read all of Lorca is to enter another world from the one we inhabit. When I first went to Spain I encountered certain phenomena that seemed inexplicable to me in the context of the Western world—in other words they did not make sense, they had no counterpart in our own culture, and they were not rational.

The so-called bullfight was a prime example. The *corrida*, it turns out, is more like the bull dance of Crete 4,000 years ago than it is like anything else in the Western world. Another was the music of southern Spain, called *flamenco*, which in many regards is more like the music of the world of the Old Testament than it is like the rest of European music. Still another was Holy Week in Sevilla, where you could still observe in the night air thick with incense and orange blossoms, candlewax and torch smoke, the celebration of Easter in ways much closer than our own to the spirit of that original palm-waving multitude rejoicing, praising God in a loud voice, and singing Hosannas as they trooped into Jerusalem.

I saw these things for the first time twenty-five years ago and was fascinated by them and studied them, but I did not understand them very well until after I read Lorca. I knew that they affected me in a powerful way, but I did not understand that they were, in fact, *all* religious expressions, not orthodoxly religious in any rational, Western, Judeo-Christian way, to be sure, but religious nonetheless. Lorca, who was the greatest cultural interpreter of all these things—these "things of Spain," as the popular phrase has it—knew that very well and explained it in no uncertain terms. He spoke of "the liturgy of the bulls, an authentic religious drama, in which, just as in the Mass, there is adoration and sacrifice of a God" (III, 316). He said it was "The only serious thing left on earth . . . the only living spectacle of antiquity in which we find all the classical essences of the most artistic peoples in the world" (Eisenberg 137).

It was precisely that old, pagan, pre-Christian element that made the ritual slaying of the bull-god so important. And the bull sacrifice was directly related in Lorca's mind to the rites of Holy Week: "The innumerable rites of Holy Friday," he wrote, "along with the most cultured *fiesta* of the bulls form the popular triumph" of Spanish culture (III, 314). For him *flamenco* was folk song submerged in an ancient people's river of voice, which he likened to a blind nightingale plaining in the infinite blue night of the Andalusian countryside (III, 207).

As I read these things, I began to understand the attraction I had felt all along, but it was his essay on *duende* that affected me most of all. *Duende*, which means "spirit," is the essence of Spanish art. Once when the great *matador* Luis Miguel *Dominguín* and Picasso were discussing art, *Dominguín* talked about *duende* as artistic inspiration: "Much has been said and much has been written about *duende*. It was Federico García Lorca's warhorse. *Duende* is not easy to explain. It's an *escalofrío*, a chill, some say. It's just that something and you have it or you don't, say others. It could be the wellspring of art, because I have realized that the most important things have no exact definition. When we are with a person or a work of art that has *duende*, no explanations are needed, and you don't have to be an expert to know rapidly and intuitively that the person or the thing has *duende*" (*Dominguín* 10).

Lorca himself was more specific. He described *duende* as "black sounds [that are] the mystery, the roots dug deep into the slime we all know, yet ignore, and through which all substance in art reaches us." It was not a question of talent but "of true living style, which is to say of blood, which is to say of very ancient culture, of creation in the act." It was that "mysterious power that we all feel but that no philosopher can explain"; it was "the spirit of the earth." It produced unknown sensations of freshness; it was a miracle; and it produced a kind of religious enthusiasm (III, 306–18). As such it was the spiritual force behind the bull rituals, behind *flamenco*, and behind the whole sense of popular culture that pervades many religious spectacles in Spain even today.

Duende is clearly Dionysian in the most ample sense of the word. Contrary to the Apollonian or rational, *duende* is poetic, nonrational, intuitive, nocturnal, lunar, and probably largely a phenomenon of the right lobe of the brain. *Duende*, demiurge, the Dionysian, call it what you will, what Lorca meant—what *duende* means—was the plumbing of the intuitive part of consciousness to its deepest levels. Lorca thought of it as a kind of religious enthusiasm or divine inspiration that had jumped from ancient Greece—especially the ancient Greece of the mystery religions—to southern Spain.

Coming to grips with the concept—should I say the mystery?—of *duende* was the hardest and the most rewarding part of this quest that I had undertaken with Lorca as my guide, my *maestro*. I had begun by assuming too cavalierly that *duende* was in part a metaphor, a poetic figure, mere literature. But I was wrong.

Research in musicology, art history, depth psychology, comparative mythology and religion, structural anthropology, biblical scholarship, ancient history and archaeology, in each case because of something Lorca had written, led me finally to understand that he was not merely being poetic. On the contrary, he was being as literal as he could in describing what we would think of as the collective unconscious as Jung explained it, or as the sacred, the mythic, or the archetypal, or what Yeats called *anima mundi*, the soul of the world. Only Lorca was describing all these things as he knew them to occur in Andalucía, and when he said the spirit of the ancient Greeks jumped from ancient Greece to the dancers and singers of Andalucía, that was precisely what he meant. His "City of the Gypsies," as he called his visionary *barrio* of moonlight and sand, was the final ephemeral flicker of a campfire built thousands of years ago.

Who was this mysterious man called Lorca, this magic and mantic and mystical man whose brief and brilliant career blazed through Spanish culture like a comet? Above all, he was the most gifted son of his own unique culture. He was, in fact (the Old Testament admonition notwithstanding), a prophet in his own land. Pariah, prodigal son, and prophet, he was so far ahead of his dismal time that the envy he inadvertently inspired may well have been a hidden motive for his assassination.

What does it mean to be this quintessential native son? What is so special about being Andalusian? Andalucía in the southern-

Lorca seated on the edge of a fountain, Granada, 1927. Courtesy of Fundación Federico García Lorca.

most part of Spain, just opposite Africa, was the first civilization in the Western world, and it developed a relatively high culture long before Greece or Italy did. Tarshish, as the Old Testament Hebrews called it, or Tartessos, as the Greeks wrote it, was the earliest independent, flourishing civilization in western Europe. In time, due to its vast mineral resources, Andalucía received,

"An Andalusian village is a living museum." Photo by Allen Josephs, 1978.

traded with, and absorbed the influence of a surprising number of mostly Oriental cultures: the megalith builders, the Bell Beaker culture; Tartessos; traders from Egypt, Crete, Turkey, and Cyprus; the Phoenicians, the Carthaginians, the Hebrews; Celts; Greeks; Romans; Visigoths; Vandals; Arabs; Berbers; Gypsies.

Yet the most remarkable aspect of Andalusian history is how little change occurred through all those centuries. As the great Spanish ethnologist, Julio Caro Baroja, eloquently expressed it, an Andalusian village is a living museum stretching from the Neolithic age to the present (II, 133). Andalucía was, in effect, frozen in time while the Western world evolved into the society of rationalistic materialism we now think of as normal. Perhaps even more striking than its remote antiquity is the extent to which that ancient culture continued to survive up to the twentieth century. Lorca was the first poet to realize the importance of this survival, and he became the greatest interpreter of that ancient subterranean river of Andalusian sensibility.

How does all this fit in with the rest of modern literature and art? Although it sounds paradoxical at first, much of modern art is not modern at all. Much of modern art is actually antimodern. A whole series of artists from Gauguin to Solzhenitsyn have turned away from rationalism, progress, modernity, and technology. Frequently they replace those things with an imitation of primitivism or a rehash of Old Testament stories and thrice-told Greek tales. Sometimes the results ring false or seem unoriginal. Lorca felt the same distrust of too much dependence on rationalism and he loved nature above all—his brief sojourn in New York angered him into a furious and prophetic denunciation of the evils of modernity. Yet Lorca did not turn to Job or Hesiod or Homer or Vergil as so many modern writers and painters have done since the Renaissance.

He did not have to because he had his own ancient culture at his disposal, one that stretched back unbroken from his childhood to the Stone Age. Instead of imitating European norms and deriving his material from Greek and Roman stories, Lorca created from within his own mythical and magical world that reverberated with all the ancient echoes his poetic genius could conjure. In that process he actually wrote, in his *Gypsy Ballads,* an original mythology; in his play *Blood Wedding,* without ever leaving the Andalusian culture he was reared in, he returned us daringly and unerringly, on the modern stage, to the dark roots of tragedy. Lorca, more than any other writer of the modern age, was able to return us to the world of the eternal present in which the sacred and the profane coexist and in which myth still has living meaning. In short, without artificiality, and with no loss of authenticity, he restored the mystery of art we had lost in the modern age.

My favorite description of Lorca was written by his friend Vicente Aleixandre a year after Lorca's death. Aleixandre survived and won the Nobel Prize in 1977.

> I have seen him in the latest nights suddenly looming over some mysterious rail, when the moon conformed with him and silvered his face; and I felt that his arms were propped in the air, but that his feet were sunken in time, in the centuries, in the remotest roots of the Spanish earth—I did not know how deep—in search of that profound wisdom that flamed in his eyes, that burned on his lips, that turned his brow incandescent with inspiration. No, he was no child then. How old, how old and how "ancient," how fabled and mythic! I mean no irreverence by this comparison: only some old *flamenco* singer, only some ancient dancer, already turned into statues of stone, could be compared to him. Only an ageless, remote Andalusian mountain, looming against a nocturnal sky, could be likened to him. . . . I spoke before of his nocturnal visage steeped in moonlight, turning almost yellow like stone, petrified as though by some ancient grief. "What ails you, my son?" the moon would seem to ask. "The earth ails me, the earth and men, human flesh and the human soul, mine and those of others, which are one with mine.". . .
>
> The poet is perhaps the being who lacks corporal limits. His long and sudden silences had about them something of the silence of a river, and in the late hour, dark as a broad river you could sense flowing, flowing, passing through him, through his body and soul, blood, remembrances, grief, the beating of other hearts and other beings that were he himself in that instant, the way the river is all the waters that give it body but not limit. The mute hour of Federico was the hour of the poet, the hour of solitude, of the generous solitude when the poet senses he is the expression of all men. (in García Lorca II, ix–xi)

Lorca in his flat on Calle Alcalá during an interview with Felipe Morales, April 17, 1936. Photo by Alfonso. Ian Gibson Archive. Courtesy of Fundacion Federico García Lorca.

I believe that in restoring for us the mystery, the awe, the sacred nature of art, Lorca became at once a great universal artist and an innovator as startlingly modern and as revolutionary as his countryman Picasso. Both were in revolt against the material world; both sought ceaselessly the innermost mystery of creation; and both daringly reached across the abyss for a new link to a world we had long left behind. That was their modernity.

In the case of Lorca there is also a wonderfully Promethean quality to his work. As he remarked to a friend, the poet Gerardo Diego, "Here it is. Look. I have the fire in my hands" (III, 401). That Promethean quality leads us beyond the bounds of what we usually take to be knowledge in any modern, rational, Judeo-Christian, Western sense. Lorca's poetry has the true gift of poetry: the invitation constantly to reexperience and reexamine everything in our existence as he, the poet as *magus*, as seer, as prophet, carries us back as no poet of our time to the nocturnal forests of the mind. Making a poem, he once wrote pointedly, was like going on "a night hunt in the most distant forest" (III, 235). He summed it all up best in the caption to one of his drawings: "Only mystery makes us live," he wrote beneath the figure. "Only mystery" (III, 1038).

ADAPTATION

Most of the poems are complete or virtually complete. Where we have made sizable deletions, we have so indicated by preceding the selection with the word from. *The order of the poems is loosely chronological, although at times for theatrical reasons we have not always followed strict chronological order. The prose selections spoken by "Lorca's voice" come from actual statements he made or letters and pieces he wrote. In some cases we have adapted the material in minor ways, but for every selection we have given our sources so the reader may easily locate the passages. None of the material was "invented" by us. It is all Lorca's.*

ONLY MYSTERY

A Chamber Theatre Script
based on the writings of
Federico García Lorca

Conceived and Compiled by Sandra Forman and Allen Josephs
Adapted for Performance by Sandra Forman
Translated by Allen Josephs

"The Señorita with the fan goes over the bridge on the cool river." Production photo from *Only Mystery: Lorca's Poetry in Performance. Left to right:* Regina David, Juan Fernandez, C. Fred Nash, Beth Sullivan, Teresa Lee, Treb Cranford, and Paula Starnes. Photo by Jan Hensley, 1988.

Only Mystery, directed by Sandra Forman, was first performed in Taylor Theatre on the campus of The University of North Carolina at Greensboro, March 30–April 1, 1988; and at the Saenger Theatre, through the University of West Florida, in Pensacola, Florida, April 9, 1988.

The original cast:

Voice of Lorca (tape)	Allen Josephs
Voice of the Child (tape)	Sandra Forman
Voice 1	Beth Sullivan
Voice 2	Juan Fernandez
Voice 3	Paula Starnes
Voice 4	Fred Nash
Voice 5	Treb Cranford
Voice 6	Teresa Lee
Voice 7	Regina David
Guitar	Mark Mazzatenta

Scenic design rendering for *Only Mystery: Lorca's Poetry in Performance.* Design by Dr. Robert C. Hansen.

Ballad of the Little Square

Federico García Lorca. *Plaza con
iglesia y fuente* [295]. Square with church
and fountain.

LORCA: *Cantan los niños*
en la noche quieta;
¡Arroyo claro,
fuente serena!

CHILD: What do you have in the *fiesta* of your divine heart?

LORCA: A tolling of bells lost in the mist.

CHILD: Now you leave us singing in the little square.
¡Arroyo claro, fuente serena!
What do you have in your hands from springtime?

25

LORCA: A rose of blood and an Easter lily.

CHILD: Moisten them with the water of the songs of old.
¡Arroyo claro, fuente serena!
What do you taste in your mouth so thirsty and red?

LORCA: The flavor of the bones of my great skull!

CHILD: Drink the still water of the songs of old.
¡Arroyo claro, fuente serena!
Why do you go so far from the little square?

LORCA: I go in search of wizards and of princesses!

CHILD: Who showed you the way of poets?

LORCA: The fountain and the stream of the songs of old.

CHILD: Do you go far, far away from the sea and from the
earth?

LORCA: My silken heart is filled with lights, with lost bells,
with lilies, and with bees, and I will go far away,
farther than those mountains, farther than the seas,
near unto the stars, to ask Christ the Lord to give me
back my soul, my ancient soul of a child,
all steeped in legends, and my plumed cap,
and my saber made of wood.

CHILD: Now you leave us singing in the little square,
¡Arroyo claro, fuente serena!
(I, 96–98)

El Campo, the Andalusian earth. Photo by Allen Josephs, 1987.

LORCA: I love the earth. I feel tied to it in all my emotions. My earliest childhood memories have a flavor of the earth. The earth, the fields, the animals of the earth, have poetic suggestions for me that few people understand. I capture them now in the same way I did as a child. (III, 599)

Paisaje

El campo
de olivos
se abre y se cierra
como un abanico.

Sobre el olivar
hay un cielo hundido
y una lluvia oscura
de luceros fríos.

Tiembla junco y penumbra
a la orilla del río.

Se riza el aire gris.

Los olivos
estan cargados
de gritos.

Una bandada
de pájaros cautivos,
que mueven sus larguísimas
colas en lo sombrío.

Landscape

v 1: The olive field
opens and closes
like a fan.

v 2: Over the grove
lie a lowering sky

v 3: and a dark rain
of cold evening stars.

v 4: Reeds and darkness tremble
along the shore of the river.

v 5: The grey air crackles.

v 6: The grove
is laden
with shrieks.

v 7: A flock
of caged birds
waving their lengthy plumes
in the darkness.
(I, 157)

Schematic Nocturne

v 6: Fennel

v 2: serpent

v 3: and reed.

v 4: Aroma

v 5: trail

v 6: and shadow.

v 1: Air

v 6: earth

v 2: and solitude.

ALL: (The scale reaches to the moon.)
(I, 274)

Little Song of Sevilla

v 5 : It was dawning
in the orange grove.
Little golden bees
were hunting for the honey.

Federico García Lorca.
*Nocturno: frutero con dos
limones* [194]. Nocturne:
Fruit bowl with two lemons.

v 6 : Where could the honey be?

v 5 : It's in that flower of blue,
Isabel.
It's in that flower
of rosemary, too.

(A little gold stool
for the Moor.
A little gilt stool
for his wife.)

It was dawning
in the orange grove.
(I, 299)

To Irene García

v 4 : Within the grove
the poplars are dancing
one along with the other.
And the *arbolé*-tree,
with its four little leaves,
is dancing with them too.

Irene!
Soon come the rains
and the snows.
Dance through the green.

Through the green green,
you and I will go.

Ay, how the water flows!
Ay, my heart!

Within the grove
the poplars are dancing
one along with the other.
And the *arbolé*-tree,
with its four little leaves,
is dancing with them too.
(I, 330)

Refrain

v 3 : March
goes flying by.

While January continues on high.

January
stays in the evening sky.

And March is but a moment below.

January.
For my old eyes.

March.
For my cool hands.
(I, 282)

August

v i : August,
   in the western sky
   counterpoints
   of peach and sugar,
   and the sun within the afternoon
   like a pit within the fruit.

The ear of corn still holds
its hard and yellow smile.

August.
The children are eating
black bread and luscious Moon.
(I, 286)

Federico García Lorca.
*Jardín con el árbol del
sol y el árbol de la
luna* [297]. Garden
with the tree of the
sun and the tree of
the moon.

People and Autumn

v7: The people were going
and autumn was coming.

The people
went to the green.
They carried cocks
and festive guitars.
To the kingdom
of the seeds.
The river dreamed,
the fountain flowed.
Leap,
hot-blooded heart!

The people
went to the green.

Autumn was coming
yellowed with stars,
scraggly birds
and concentric waves.
Above the starched shirtfront,
the head.
Stop,
heart of wax!

The people were going
and autumn was coming.
(I, 332)

Federico García
Lorca. *Cabeza
desdoblada de
Pierrot* [228.2].
Pierrot's head
unfolded.

from *Nocturne at the Window*

1.

v2 : High goes the moon.
Low runs the wind.

> (My long looks
> explore the sky.)

Moon on top of the water.
Moon beneath the wind.

> (My short looks
> explore the ground.)

The voices of two little girls
approaching. Effortlessly I go
from the moon on the water
to the one up in the sky.

2.

An arm of the night
comes in through
my window.

A great dark arm
wearing bangles of water.

Above the crystal blue
my soul pretends it's a river.

The moments wounded
by the clock . . . are passing.

3.

I lean my head out of the window
and see how the blade of the wind
intends to chop it off.

Into this invisible guillotine
I've placed the sightless head
of all of my desires.

A sudden scent of lemon
filled the boundless moment
while the wind turned into gauzy blooms.
(I, 291–93)

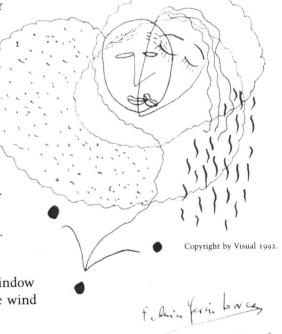

Authentic details: An Andalusian flock. Photo by Allen Josephs, 1987.

LORCA: My whole childhood was the *pueblo*. Shepherds, fields, the sky, solitude, simplicity above all. It always surprises me when people think the things in my work are my own inventions. The audaciousness of the poet. No. They are authentic details that to most people seem very strange. (III, 622)

I don't conceive of poetry as an abstraction but as a very real existing thing which has passed close to me. All the people in my poems have actually existed. (III, 671)

Chinese Song in Europe

v 7 : The *señorita*
with the fan
goes over the bridge
on the cool river.

The gentlemen
with their smocks
are looking at the bridge
with no railings.

The *señorita*
with the fan
and flounces
seeks a husband.

The gentlemen
are married
to tall blondes
with white speech.

The crickets are singing
in the west.

(The *señorita*
goes toward the green.)

The crickets sing
under the flowers.

(The gentlemen
head for the north.)
(I, 297–98)

Federico García Lorca.
Casa con torre [296].
House with tower.

35

Silly Song

v 5 : *Mamá.*
I want to be made of silver.

v 7 : Son,
You would be very cold.

v 5 : *Mamá.*
I want to be made of water.

v 7 : Son,
you would be very cold.

v 5 : *Mamá.*
Embroider me on your pillow.

v 7 : Oh, yes!
Right this minute!
(I, 304)

from *Song*

v 6 : The girl with the lovely face
is picking the olive tree.

v 7 : The wind that woos the towers
takes her around the waist.

v 2 : Four riders come passing by
on Andalusian ponies,
with suits of blue and green
and long dark capes.
"Come to Córdoba, *muchacha!*"

W O M E N : The girl pays no attention.

v 4 : Then came three *toreros*
narrow at the waist
with orange suits of lights
and swords of ancient silver.
"Come to Sevilla, *muchacha!*"

W O M E N : The girl pays no attention.

v 5 : When the afternoon turned purple
and the light began to dim
there came a youth with roses
and myrtles of the moon.
"Come to Granada, *muchacha!*"

W O M E N : The girl pays no attention.

v 1 : The girl with the lovely face
    continues picking olives,

v 6 : with the great gray arm of the wind
    tucked closely about her waist.
    (I, 315–16)

Federico García
Lorca. *Dama
española* [114].
Spanish Lady.

37

Corridor

v3: Through the high corridors
two gentlemen were walking.

ALL: (New
sky.
Sky
of blue!)

v3: . . . two gentlemen were walking
who once were white monks.

ALL: (Middle
sky.
Sky
of purple!)

v3: . . . two gentlemen were walking
who once were fierce hunters.

ALL: (Old
sky.
Sky
of gold!)

v3: . . . two gentlemen were walking
who once were . . .

ALL: Night.
(I, 262)

Serenade

v2: Along the shore of the river
the night is beginning to bathe,
and in the breasts of Lolita
the bouquets are dying of love.

ALL: The bouquets are dying of love.

v2: The night is singing naked
across the bridges of March.
Lolita washes her body
with briny water and nard.

ALL: The bouquets are dying of love.

  V2: The night of *anís* and silver
     glistens above the rooves.
     Silver of streams and mirrors.
     Anís of your snowy thighs.

ALL: The bouquets are dying of love.
    (I, 354)

Federico García Lorca.
Agua sexual [290.5].
Sexual water.

LORCA: When I was a child I lived in an atmosphere full of nature. Like all children I gave everything—pieces of furniture, objects, trees, stones—their own personality. I talked to them and I loved them. There were some poplars in the backyard of my house. One afternoon it occurred to me that the poplars were singing. The wind, as it passed through the branches, made a noise that varied in tones that struck me as musical. And I used to spend hours singing with my voice the song of the poplars.

One day I stopped, amazed. Someone was saying my
name, separating the syllables as though spelling:
FE DE RI CO. I looked everywhere and saw no one.
Still in my ears my name kept ringing. After listening
for a long time, I figured it out. The branches from an
old poplar tree were rubbing together and making a
monotonous moaning sound that seemed to me to be
my name. (III, 598)

De otro modo

La hoguera pone al campo de la tarde
unas astas de ciervo enfurecido.
Todo el valle se tiende. Por sus lomos,
caracolea el vientecillo.

El aire cristaliza bajo el humo.
—Ojo de gato triste y amarillo—.
Yo, en mis ojos, paseo por las ramas.
Las ramas se pasean por el río.

Llegan mis cosas esenciales.
Son estribillos de estribillos.
Entre los juncos y la baja tarde,
¡qué raro que me llame Federico!

Federico García Lorca.
Camino y bosque [87].
Road and trees.

In Another Way

v4: The bonfire flickers on the field of the afternoon
like the horns of a furious stag.
The whole valley reclines as the wind
caracoles lightly over the ridges.

The air, like the eye of a sad, yellow cat,
crystallizes under the smoke.
I, in my eyes, walk along the branches.
The branches parade down the river.

My essential things have come.
Refrains within refrains.
Among the reeds and the fading afternoon,
how strange they call me Federico!
(I, 381)

from *Wellspring*   v7: I encrusted myself in the ancient poplar
with sadness and with desire.

My spirit melted into the leaves.
My blood turned to sap.

In the wide winter sunset
I twisted my branches
savoring the unknown rhythms
on the frozen breeze.

The landscape and the earth were lost.
Only the sky remained.
And I heard the soft murmur of the stars
and the breathing of the mountains.

I raised my branches toward the sky.

And felt the bubbling of springs
the way I heard them when I was human.
It was the same flowing full of music
and unknown science.

v4: "Become the nightingale,"

v7:   said a voice lost
in the dead distance,
and a torrent of warm stars
sprouted through the guarded breast of night.
(I, 126–27)

Little Song of the First Desire

v6: In the green morning
I wanted to be a heart.

ALL: Heart.

v6: And in the ripened afternoon
I wanted to be a nightingale.

ALL: Nightingale.

v6: (Soul,
turn orange.
Soul,
turn the color of love.)

In the living morning
I wanted to be I.

ALL: Heart.

v6: And in the dying afternoon
I wanted to be my voice.

ALL: Nightingale.

v6: (Soul,
turn orange!
Soul,
turn the color of love!)
(I, 369)

It Died at Dawn

v2: Night of four moons
and one tree only,
with one shadow only
and one bird only.

I seek in my flesh
the marks of your lips.
The wellspring kisses the wind
without touching.

I carry the No you gave me
in the palm of my hand,
like a lemon of wax
nearly white.

Night of four moons
and one tree only.
On the point of a needle
is my love. Whirling!
(I, 343)

It Is True

v1: Oh what trouble it costs me
    to love you the way I do!

Your love makes the air hurt,
and my heart.
Even my hat.

Who's going to buy from me now
this little ribbon I have
or this sadness of white linen
to make into handkerchiefs?

Oh what trouble it costs me
to love you as I do!
(I, 314)

Prelude

v5: The poplars disappear
    but leave us their reflection.

v3: The poplars disappear
    but they leave us the wind.

v5: The wind is wrapped in a shroud
    laid out beneath the sky.

v3: But it has left its echoes
    floating over the rivers.

v5: A world of fireflies
    has invaded my memories.

v3: And a tiny heart
    starts budding from my fingers.
    (I, 376)

Federico García Lorca.
*Muchacha granadina en un
jardín* [72]. Granada
girl in a garden.

from *Dead Poplar*

v4: Old poplar!
    You fell
    into the mirror
    of the sleeping pool.
    I saw you falling
    in the twilight
    and I write your
        elegy
    which is also
        my own.
    (I, 108–9)

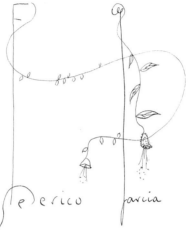

LORCA: Every step that an artist takes towards the tower of his
       perfection is at the cost of the struggle he maintains
       with a force, a spirit we call *duende*. (III, 308) The
       great artists of southern Spain know that no real
       emotion is possible unless there is *duende*. (III, 309) It
       is not a matter of ability but of blood; of ancient
       culture. (III, 307) The *duende* has to be aroused in the
       distant-most chambers of the blood. (III, 308) The
       duende surges up from the soles of the feet. All that
       has black sound has *duende*. These "black sounds" are
       the mystery known to all of us, ignored by all of us.
       This mysterious power that everyone feels but that no
       philosopher has explained is in fact the spirit of the
       earth. (III, 307)

       The *duende* does not appear if it sees no possibility of
       death. (III, 314) In every other country death is an
       ending. It arrives and the curtains are closed. *¡En
       Espana, NO!* (III, 312)

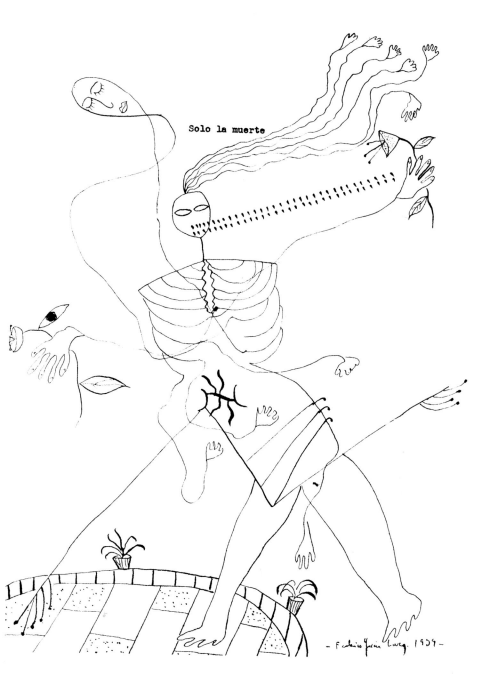

Solo la muerte

Opposite: Federico García Lorca. *Firma con luna reflejada* [196]. Signature with reflected moon. *Above:* Federico García Lorca. *Sólo la muerte* [290.2]. Only death. © Visual 1992.

La guitarra

Empieza el llanto
de la guitarra.
Se rompen las copas
de la madrugada.
Empieza el llanto
de la guitarra.
Es inútil callarla.
Es imposible
callarla.

Llora monótona
como llora el agua,
como llora el viento
sobre la nevada.
Es imposible
callarla.

Llora por cosas lejanas.
Arena del Sur caliente
que pide camelias blancas.
Llora flecha sin blanco,
la tarde sin mañana,
y el primer pájaro muerto
sobre la rama.

¡Oh, guitarra!
Corazón malherido
por cinco espadas.

Federico García Lorca.
Guitarra [118]. Guitar.

The Guitar

v2: The lament of the guitar
is beginning.

v1: The goblets of dawn
shatter.

v7: The lament of the guitar
is beginning.

v4: It's useless to stop it.

v5: It's impossible
to stop it.

v6: It weeps monotonous
as the water weeps,
as the wind weeps
over the snow.

v5: It's impossible
to stop it.

v3: It weeps for distant things.

v4: Hot sands of the South
seeking white camelias.

v1: It weeps arrows with no mark,

v3: evening with no morning,

v6: and the first bird dead
upon the branch.

ALL: Oh, *guitarra!*
Heart wounded
by five swords.
(I, 158)

Malagueña

v2: Death goes in
and death goes out
of the tavern.

Black horses
and sinister people
roam the hidden trails
of the guitar.

And there is a scent of salt
and woman's blood
in the febrile flowers
on the beach.

Death goes in
and death goes out
and death goes out
and death goes in
to the tavern.
(I, 211)

Federico García Lorca.
Danza macabra [153].
Dance of death.

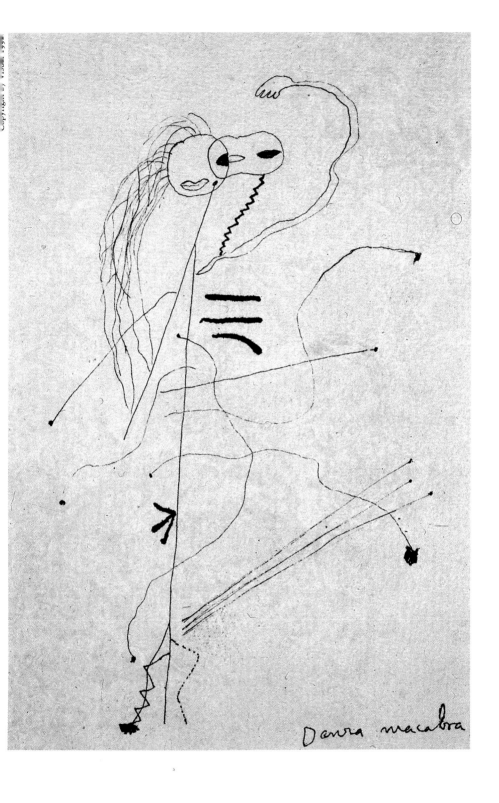

Danza macabra

Camino

WOMEN: A hundred riders in mourning.

    V6: I wonder where they're going
         against the lowering sky
         of the orange grove?

    V7: They're not going to Córdoba

    V1: nor to Sevilla.

    V3: Nor to Granada
         sighing for the sea.

    V6: Their sleepwalking horses
         will take them
         to the labyrinth of crosses
         where songs shiver.

    V7: With seven swords of sorrow
         I wonder where they're going,

    V1: the hundred Andalusian riders

    V3: passing through the orange grove?
         (I, 190)

Federico García Lorca. *Paso
de la virgen de los Dolores*
[65]. Palanquin of the Virgin
of Sorrows.

Song of the Rider (1860)

V2: In the black moon
of the *bandoleros*
spurs are singing.

ALL: Black horse.
Where do you take your dead rider?

V5: . . . The hard spurs
of the motionless bandit
who lost his reins.

ALL: Cold horse.
What a scent of knife-blooms!

V2: In the black moon
the side of the *sierra*
is bleeding.

ALL: Black horse.
Where do you take your dead rider?

V5: Night spurs
her black flanks
with the stars.

ALL: Cold horse.
What a scent of knife-blooms!

V2: In the black moon,
a scream
and a long horn of fire.

ALL: Black horse.
Where do you take your dead rider?
(I, 307–8)

Song of the Rider

v4: Córdoba.
   Far away and alone.

   Black horse, big moon,
   olives in my saddlebag.
   Even though I know the way
   I'll never get to Córdoba.

   Over the plain, into the wind,
   black horse, red moon.
   Death is watching me
   from the towers of Córdoba.

   Ay! The long road!
   Ay! My brave horse!
   Ay! Death is waiting for me
   before I get to Córdoba!

   Córdoba.
   Far away and alone.
   (I, 313)

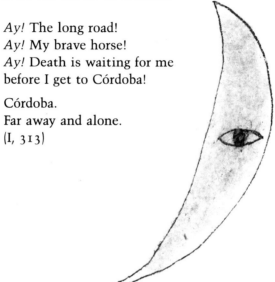

Federico García Lorca. From
*Dedicatoria a Emilia Llanos
y media luna en azul* [234.1].
From Dedication to Emilia
Llanos and half moon in blue.
© Visual 1992.

LORCA: The Gypsy is the most elevated, the most profound, the most aristocratic type in my country, the most representative of our way of being and the one who safeguards the embers, the blood and the alphabet of Andalusian and universal truth. (III, 340)

From Jerez to Cádiz, ten clans of the purest lineage jealously guard the glorious traditions of the *flamenco* way of life. (III, 658)

In my Gypsy ballads there is only one character as large and dark as a summer sky, one character which is *la pena*—the pain, the suffering, the grief of Andalucía—which seeps through the marrow of bones and the sap of trees; it is the struggle of a loving intelligence with the surrounding mystery that it cannot comprehend. (III, 340)

La pena, the pain, of Soledad Montoya is the root of the Andalusian people. It is a desire with no object, a fierce love of nothing specific, with the certainty that death is breathing behind the door.

Soledad Montoya is the personification of the *pena* without recourse, helpless, of *pena negra*, the black pain from which there is no escape but death. (III, 344)

Summer storm in Andalucía.
Photo by Allen Josephs, 1987.

Ballad of the Black Pain

v2: The beaks of the cocks
peck in search of the dawn
as Soledad Montoya
descends the dark mountain,
her flesh the color of copper,
smelling of horses and shadow,
the smoky anvils of her breasts
moaning rounded songs.

"Soledad, who are you asking for,
alone and at this hour?"

v6: "Never mind who I'm asking for.
What business is it of yours?
I seek what I seek,
My happiness and my self."

v2: "Soledad of my sorrows,
the horse that breaks away
finds only the sea
to be swallowed by the waves."

v6: "Don't tell me about the sea.
For the *pena negra* spurts
from deep within the olive groves
beneath the rustling murmur of leaves."

v2: "Soledad, what pain you suffer!
What pitiful bitter pain!
The tears you weep are lemon drops
sour in your mouth from waiting."

v6: "What terrible pain! I pace
wildly through my house
from kitchen to bedroom and back,
my long tresses trailing to the floor.
What pain! My clothes and my flesh
are turning black as jet.
Ay, my gowns of fine linen!
Ay, my thighs of red poppy!"

v2: "Soledad, bathe your body
in the water of the larks,
and let your heart be at peace
Soledad Montoya."

Down below the river sings,
bearing the sky and leaves.
Yellow pumpkin flowers
crown the breaking light.
Oh pain of the Gypsies!
Pure and solitary pain.
Oh pain of hidden source
and distant dawn!
(I, 408–9)

Federico García Lorca. *Soledad Montoya* [240.4]. Soledad Montoya. © Visual 1992.

Federico García Lorca. *Gitano malísimo* [158]. Very bad gypsy. © Visual 1992.

LORCA: There is a silent struggle latent in Andalucía and in all of Spain among groups that attack each other without knowing why—for mysterious reasons, for a look, for a rose, because a man is unexpectedly bitten on the cheek by an insect, because of a love affair two centuries ago. (III, 343)

Knife-fight

v7: Halfway down the ravine
knife blades from Albacete,
bright with rivals' blood,
shine like a school of fish.
A harsh card-edged light
silhouettes, against the green,
furious rearing horses
and profiles of their riders.
On the bough of an ancient olive tree
two old women are weeping.
The fighting-bull of the brawl
scrambles straight up the walls.
Dark-skinned angels are bringing
handkerchiefs and melting snow.
Angels with blades for wings,
knife blades from Albacete.
Juan Antonio from Montilla
falls dying down the slope,
his body laced with lilies,
pomegranates on his head.
Now he rides a cross of fire
down the highway of death.
The judge and the *Guardia Civil*
come through the olive groves.
The spilt blood is moaning
the mute song of the snake.

v4: "Officers of the *Guardia Civil*,
it's the same old story again:
Four Romans have died here
and five Carthaginians."

v7: The maddened afternoon thick
with fig trees and burning murmurs
faints in the wounded thighs of the riders.
And dark-skinned angels are flying
through the air of the western sky.
Angels with hearts of olive oil
and long black braided hair.
(I, 398–99)

LORCA: The true Gypsies have never stolen anything. The real
Gypsies are not people who go from *pueblo* to *pueblo*
all dirty and dressed in rags . . . the real Gypsy is the
purest and most authentic thing in Andalucía.
(Rodrigo 348)

But what clatter of hooves and reins sounds
throughout Jaén and along the *sierras* of Almería? The
Civil Guard is coming. (III, 346)

The *Guardia Civil* comes and destroys the city of the
Gypsies. (III, 901)

Ballad of the Spanish Civil Guard

v4: Black are the horses.

v2: Black the horseshoes.

v5: Ink stains and spots of wax
gleam on their capes.

v4: Their skulls are made of lead;
therefore they never weep.

v2: With souls of patent leather
they ride the roads
hunched over and nocturnal,
demanding everywhere they go
a dark rubber silence
and sand grains of fear.

v5: They go anywhere they choose
and hide within their heads
a vague astronomy
with pistol constellations.

WOMEN: O city of the Gypsies!

v3: Banners at every corner,

v1: pumpkins in the moonlight,

v3: cherries preserved in jars.

WOMEN: O city of the Gypsies!

v6: Who could see you and forget?

v7: City of musk and sorrow,

v6: city of cinnamon towers.

v1: When night began to fall,
    night that nightened the night,
    the Gypsies within their forges
    hammered out arrows and suns.
    A single wounded stallion
    knocked at every door.
    Cocks of crystal crowed
    in Jerez de la Frontera.
    The naked wind whipped
    around the corner by surprise,
    in the silver nightening light,
    night that nightened the night.

v7: The Virgin and San José,
    having lost their castanets,
    are trying to find the Gypsies
    to see if they can help.
    The Virgin, very festive,
    looks like the Mayor's wife,
    her dress of chocolate paper,
    her necklaces strung with almonds.
    San José's arms are dancing
    beneath his cape of silk.
    Behind him goes Pedro Domecq
    with three sultans from Persia.
    The half moon dreams in ecstasy,
    like a stork above its nest.
    Banners and flickering lamps
    cast a spell on the darkened rooves.
    Dancing girls with no hips
    sob within the mirrors.
    Water and shadow, shadow and water
    at Jerez de la Frontera.

WOMEN: O city of the Gypsies!

v3: Banners at every corner.
    Put out your green lights,
    the *Guardia Civil* is coming.

WOMEN: O city of the Gypsies!

v6: Who could see you and forget?
Leave her far from this sea
with no combs to shine in her hair.

v2: They advance two by two
towards the city in *fiesta.*
A whisper of immortelles
invades the bandoliers.
Advancing two by two
in a double nocturne of capes.
To them the heavens seem
a glittering showcase of spurs.

v4: The city, free of fear,
has multiplied its doors.
Forty Civil Guards
storm through to plunder.
The clocks all stopped at once,
and the cognac inside its bottles
pretended not to notice.

v5: A flight of anguished cries
took wing among the weather vanes.
Sabers hacked the breezes
trampled beneath the hooves.

v2: Through the streets of shadow
old Gypsy women fled,
dragging sleepy horses
and clutching crocks of coins.

v5: Up through the steepening streets
climb the sinister capes,
leaving eddies full of blades
whirling briefly in their wake.

v6: At the gate of Bethlehem
the Gypsies are gathered together.
San José, covered with wounds,
wraps a girl with a shroud.

v3: Sharp rifle reports
clatter through the night.

v1: The Virgin heals the children
with saliva from the stars.

Federico García
Lorca. *Suplicio
del patriarca
San José* [142].
Suffering of
the patriarch
Saint Joseph.

v6: But the *Guardia Civil* advances
spreading bonfires in its path

v3: and sending young Imagination,
naked, up in flames.

v7: Rosa de los Camborios
moans sitting in her door
with both her severed breasts
placed upon a tray.

v1: Other girls are running away
pursued by their streaming braids
as black gunpowder roses
burst in the smoking air.

v4: When every roof
was a rut in the earth,
daybreak shrugged her shoulders
turning a long profile of stone.

ALL: O city of the Gypsies!

v4: The Civil Guard departs
through a tunnel of silence
as the flames burn you down.

ALL: O city of the Gypsies!
Who could see you and forget?

LORCA: Let them find you in my mind.
Moonlight playing on the sand.
(I, 426–30)

Federico García Lorca.
Material nupcial [290.6].
Nuptial material.

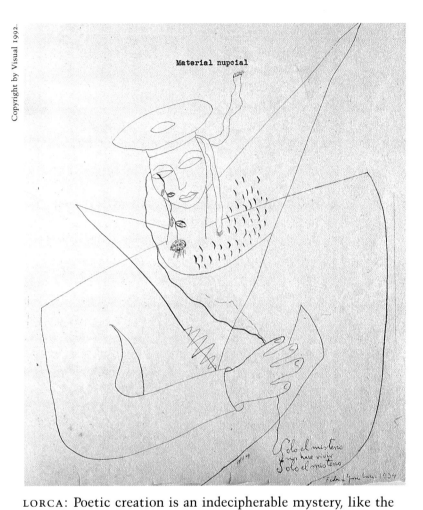

LORCA: Poetic creation is an indecipherable mystery, like the mystery of man. (III, 681) Each thing has its own mystery and poetry is the mystery all things have. (III, 671) The imagination fixes and gives clear life to fragments of the invisible reality where man abides. (III, 259) Through poetry man more quickly approaches the edge where the philosopher and the mathematician turn their backs in silence. (III, 343)

Sólo el misterio nos hace vivir. Sólo el misterio.

Only mystery makes us live. Only mystery. (III, 1038)

Zorongo

(Sung)

1.

v2 : *Tengo los ojos azules,*
tengo los ojos azules
y el corazoncillo igual
que la cresta de la lumbre.

2.

De noche me salgo al patio
y me harto de llorar
de ver que te quiero tanto
y tú no me quieres na.

3.

Esta gitana está loca,
pero loquita de atar,
que lo que sueña de noche
quiere que sea verdad.

4.

Las manos de mi cariño
te están bordando una capa
con agremán de alhelíes
y con esclavina de agua.
Cuando fuiste novio mío
por la primavera blanca,
los cascos de tu caballo
cuatro sollozos de plata.

La luna es un pozo chico,
las flores no valen nada,
lo que valen son tus brazos
cuando de noche me abrazan,
lo que valen son tus brazos
cuando de noche me abrazan.
(Stanzas 1–3 in I, 1130;
stanza 4 and music in II,
1174–76)

Casida *of the Branches*

v i : In the poplar groves of Tamarit
leaden dogs have gathered,
waiting for the branches to fall,
waiting for them to break by themselves.

At Tamarit there's an apple tree
with an apple full of sobs.
A nightingale muffles its sighs
and a pheasant drives them through dust.

But the branches are happy,
the branches are like we are.
Not thinking of rain, like trees
they've suddenly fallen asleep.

Sitting with water up to their knees,
two valleys waited for autumn.
Darkness fell like an elephant's step,
pushing the branches and trunks.

In the poplar groves of Tamarit
there are many children with veiled faces,
waiting for my branches to fall,
waiting for them to break by themselves.
(I, 591)

Federico García Lorca.
Animal fabuloso
dirigiéndose a una casa
[166]. Imaginary animal
heading for a house.

Gacela *of Dark Death*

v 5 : I want to sleep the sleep of apples,
to get away from the tumult of cemeteries.
I want to sleep the sleep of that child
who wished to cut out his heart at sea.

I don't want them to tell me again
that the dead don't lose their blood,
that the rotting mouth still begs for water.
I don't want to know how the weeds martyr us
nor how before dawn the moon
works with her serpent's mouth.

I want to sleep a moment,
a moment, a minute, a century;
but all must know I haven't died;
that there's a stable of gold in my lips;
that I'm the small friend of
   the West Wind;
that I'm the huge shadow
   of my tears.

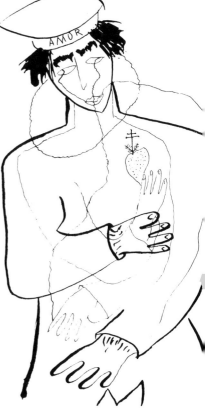

Cover me by dawn with a veil,
for dawn will throw me handfuls
   of ants,
and soak my shoes in hard water
so the scorpion's claw will slip.

Because I want to sleep the
   sleep of apples
to learn a lament that will
   cleanse me of dirt;
because I want to live with
   that dark child
who wished to cut out his
   heart at sea.
(I, 581)

Gacela *of the Flight*

v 3 : I've been lost at sea many times
with my ears full of fresh cut flowers,
with my tongue full of love and agony.
I've been lost at sea many times,
the way I'm lost in the hearts of certain children.

No one kissing at night fails to feel
the smile of the faceless people,
and no one touching a newborn child
forgets the motionless skulls of horses.

Because roses seek through the forehead
a hard landscape of bone,
and the hands of man make no sense
except imitating roots under ground.

The way I'm lost
in the hearts of
certain children
I've been lost at sea
many times.
Ignoring the water,
I'm seeking
a death of light to
consume me.
(I, 583)

Left: Federico
García Lorca.
*Marinero del
"amor"* [188].
Sailor of "love."
Right: Federico
García Lorca.
*Marinero con
columna* [202].
Sailor with
column.

Gacela *of Desperate Love*

v7: Night doesn't want to fall
so that you can't come
and I can't go.

But I will go
even though a scorpion sun devour my brain.

And you will come
with your tongue burnt by a rain of salt.

Day doesn't want to break
so that you can't come
and I can't go.

But I will go
leaving the toads my mangled carnation.

And you will come
through the turbid sewers of darkness.

Night doesn't want to fall
and day doesn't want to break
so that I might die for you
and you might die for me.
(I, 575)

Gacela *of the Memory of Love*

v 4 : Don't take away your memory.
Leave it alone in my heart,

trembling like a white cherry tree
martyred in January.

A wall of bad dreams
separates me from the dead.

I will give a fresh lily's pain
for a heart of plaster.

All night long in the garden
my eyes, like two dogs.

All night long eating
poisoned candied fruit.

Sometimes the wind
is a tulip of fear,

and winter's dawn is
a tulip of disease.

A wall of bad dreams
separates me from the dead.

Grass covers in silence
the gray valley of your body.

Beside the archway where we met
a hemlock tree is growing.

But leave me the memory of you,
leave it alone in my heart.
(I, 579–80)

Left: Federico
García Lorca.
Rostro con flechas
[211]. Face with
arrows. *Above:*
Federico García
Lorca. *Rostro de
las dos flechas*
[212]. Face of two
arrows.

Casida *of the Impossible Hand*

v6: All I want is a hand,
  a wounded hand, if it's possible.
  All I want is a hand
  though I spend a thousand nights with no bed.

It would be a pale lily of lime,
it would be a dove tied to my heart,
it would be my angel absolutely forbidding
the moon to shine on the night of my dying.

All I want is that hand
for the daily rituals and the white shroud of my
  agony.
All I want is that hand
to have one wing of my death.

All the rest will pass.
Already a nameless blush. Perpetual star.
All the rest is otherness; a sad wind
as flocks of leaves flee past.
(I, 594)

Federico García Lorca. *Manos cortadas* [213]. Severed hands.
© Visual 1992.

LORCA: Paris made an enormous impression on me; London even more, and now New York is like a great hammer blow to the head. Paris and London are two country towns, two *pueblecitos,* compared to this vibrating and maddening Babylonia . . . this immense Babel. (Maurer 35, 37)

In New York is man's immense struggle with the edges of the skyscrapers, under an indifferent sky; his intense solitude under the thousands of immutable windows and the glitter of the luminous billboards of Broadway. (De la Guardia 91)

The English have brought here a civilization without roots. They have raised buildings and more buildings, but they have not dug into the earth. (III, 675)

I sketch the gigantic city with four strokes: an extra-human architecture, a furious rhythm, geometry, and anguish. I bring you a bitter and living poetry that will lash open your eyes. (De la Guardia 90–91)

Chrysler Building,
New York City.
Photo by Browning
Studios. Courtesy of
the New York
Historical Society.

Dawn

v2: Dawn in New York
has four columns of slime
and a whirlwind of black pigeons
that splatter in the putrid water.

v5: Dawn in New York moans
through the high-rising stairs
seeking along the edges
the traces of anguished flowers.

v4: Dawn comes and there is no mouth to receive her,
there's no morning nor possible hope.
Now and then furious swarms of coins
ravage and devour long lost boys and girls.

v2: The first on the streets understand in their bones,
for them no paradise, no unfolding loves;

v5: knowingly they go to the swamp of numbers and laws,
to artless games, to fruitless sweat.

v4: Light is buried in chains and noises,
in the menace of science, rootless and impudent.
Through the neighborhoods people wander sleeplessly
like recent survivors of a shipwreck of blood.
(I, 485)

Federico García Lorca.
El hi [178]. The *hi.*

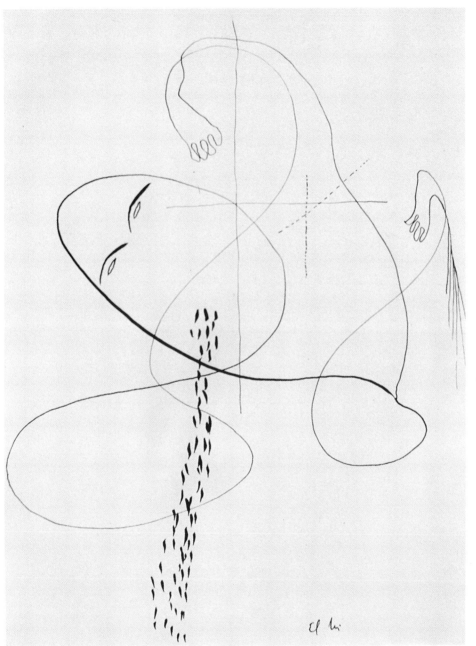

Murder

(Two voices at dawn. Riverside Drive.)

v7: "*What happened?*"

v1: "A slash in the cheek.
That's all!

v3: A fingernail that digs into the stem.

v6: A pinpoint that dives
till it reaches the roots of the cry.

v5: And the sea ceases to move."

v7: "*What? What happened?*"

v6: "Just like that."

v7: "*Stop! Like that?*"

v1: "Yes.
The heart came out by itself."

v7: "*¡Ay, ay de mí!*"
(I, 477)

LORCA: My poems about New York make contact between my
own poetic world and the poetic world of New York.
There, between these worlds, drift the sad people of
Africa lost in North America. Other than the art of the
negro, there is nothing in the United States but
machinery and automation. Their sadness has become
the spiritual axis of America. (III, 502)

Street scene in Harlem, 1920s.
S. Forman Archive.

from *The King of Harlem*

v2: With a spoon
he dug out the crocodiles' eyes
and beat on the butts of the monkeys
with a spoon.

An old man covered with mushrooms
went where the black men weep
while the king's spoon crackled.

Time to cross the bridges
to get to the black man's blush.

Time to kill the blond liquor salesman
and beat the little jewesses
trembling full of bubbles,
so the king of Harlem can sing with his hosts.

ALL: *Ay, Harlem! Ay, Harlem! Ay, Harlem!*

v2: No anguish like your reddened oppression,
your shuddering blood in its dark eclipse,
your garnet rage, deaf and dumb in the dark,
your prisoner king trapped in his janitor's suit.

The night had a rift and motionless marble lizards.
The American girls
kept babies and coins in their wombs,
while the boys awakened in a faint.
They are the ones.

That night the king of Harlem
using the hardest of spoons
gouged out the crocodiles' eyes
and beat on the monkeys' butts
with a spoon.
Black men wept in a confusion
of umbrellas and golden suns.

ALL: *Negros, negros, negros, negros.*

v2: Blood has no doors in your night turned upside down.
No blush of blood. Furious blood beneath the skin,
living blood on the dagger's thorn.
Blood that seeks on a thousand roads ashen dusty death.

Federico García Lorca. *Personaje quimérico
con frac y paraguas* [9]. Chimerical character
with topcoat and umbrella. © Visual 1992.

It is the blood that is coming everywhere,
that will come over the rooves and terraces
to burn the chlorophyll of blond women,
to wail at the feet of sleepless beds,
to explode in a dull yellow
and tobacco-colored dawn.

Through the sapient silence
the waiters and the cooks
and those who lick the millionaires' wounds
search the streets for their king.

ALL: *Negros, negros, negros, negros.*

V2: No snake, no zebra, no mule
ever went white before it died.
Wait beneath the vegetable shadow of your king
for the hemlocks, the thistles, and the thorns
to crack the distant rooves.

Then, *negros.* Then. Then
you can dance finally with no doubts
while the bristling flowers
murder our Moses almost at the reeds of heaven.

Ay, Harlem in disguise!
Ay, Harlem,
threatened by a mob of headless suits!
Your murmur reaches me.
Your murmur reaches me
through the tree-trunks, through the elevators,
through the dead horses and the petty crimes,
through your great and desperate king
whose whiskers reach to the sea.
(I, 459–63)

LORCA: Coney Island is a great fair where every Sunday in the summer more than a million creatures come. They drink, they shout, they eat, they writhe about leaving a sea full of newspapers and the streets littered with tin cans, cigarette butts, bites of food and shoes with broken heels.

No one can imagine the loneliness a Spaniard feels there; because if you fall you will be trampled and if you slide into the water, they will throw lunch wrappers on you. (III, 353)

An aerial view of Coney Island.
S. Forman Archive.

89

from *Landscape of the Vomiting Multitudes*

v 5 : Coney Island nightfall
    and the fat lady was out in front
    yanking up roots and wetting the drums;
    the fat lady
    turning a dying octopus inside out.

The fat lady, enemy of the moon,
hurried through the streets and empty buildings
leaving pigeon skulls in the corners,
rousing the ghosts of bygone banquets,
summoning a demon of bread from the windswept sky,
and slipping a desire for light into underground passages.

These are cemeteries, I know. They're graveyards
and kitchens of grief buried in the sand;
they're the dead, the pheasants and apples of some other
    time
that push up against our throats.

Murmurs come from the jungle of vomit
and vacant women with children of wax
and fermenting trees and tireless waiters
serving plates of salt.
It's no use, son. Vomit! There's nothing else to do.

This is not soldier's vomit on the breasts of a whore,
nor the vomit of a cat that swallowed a frog by accident.
These are the dead scratching with fingers of clay
at the stony doors where all things rot.

The fat lady was out in front
with the crowds from the boats and the bars.

Vomit delicately dribbled on the drums
among certain girls of blood
seeking the protection of the moon.
Oh, my God! Oh, my God! Oh, my God!
This look that once was mine
is now mine no longer,
this look that trembles naked in alcohol.
I defend myself with this look
that springs from waves where dawn never dares;
I, poet with no arms, lost
in this vomiting multitude
with no effusive horse to chop away
the thick moss from my head.

And the fat lady was still out in front . . .
(I, 473–74)

Federico García Lorca. *Muerte de Santa
Rodegunda* [161]. Death of Saint Rodegunda.

LORCA: New York seemed horrible to me. That's precisely why
I went there. (III, 991) I denounce life in New York
because I come from the *campo,* the countryside, and I
believe that the most important thing is not man. (III,
356) *Nueva York* is terrible. Something monstrous.
New York is the greatest lie in the world. New York is
a jungle with machines. (III, 675)

from *New York: Office and Denunciation*

v 1 : Beneath the multiplications
there is a drop of duck's blood.

v 3 : Beneath the divisions,
there is a drop of sailor's blood.

v 6 : Beneath the additions, a river of tender blood;
a river that flows singing
through the tenements and slums,

v 7 : a river of silver, cement or breeze
in the fake dawn of New York.

v 4 : The mountains exists, I know.
And eye-glasses for wisdom, I know.
But I have not come to gaze at the sky.
I have come to see the turbid blood,
the blood that sweeps machines over the falls
and carries souls to the tongue of the cobra.

v 1 : Every day in New York they slaughter

v 2 : four million ducks,

v 3 : five million pigs,

v 5 : two thousand doves for the pleasure of the dying

v 6 : one million cows,

v 1 : one million lambs,

v 7 : and two million roosters
that shatter the heavens to pieces.

v 2 : It's better to sob and sharpen the switchblade

v 3 : or murder the dogs in maddening chases,

v 1 : than to resist at dawn
the interminable trains of milk,

v 2 : the interminable trains of blood,

v 3 : the trains of handtied roses
bound by the peddlers of perfume.

v 5 : The ducks and the doves,
and the pigs and the lambs
shed drops of their blood
beneath the multiplications,

Federico
García Lorca.
*Autorretrato
en Nueva
York* [171].
Self-portrait
in New York.

v6: and the terrible bellows of stampeded cattle
fill the valley with weeping

ALL: where the Hudson flows, drunk on oil.

v4: I denounce all those
who ignore the other side.
I denounce that unredeemable half
that raises mountains of cement
where the hearts of animals
beat in oblivion,
and where we all will fall
in the ultimate orgy of jackhammers.

ALL: I spit in your faces!

v2: This is not hell; it's the street.

v5: It's not death; it's a fruit-stand.

v7: There is a world of broken rivers and unreachable
distances
in the cat's paw smashed by the motorist.

v1: And I hear the song of the worm
in the hearts of many young girls.

v3: Rust,

v6:   fermentation,

v7:   trembling earth.

v4: You are earth yourself floating among the numbers in the
office.
What can I do, rearrange the landscape?
Arrange the lovers who turn into photographs
and later are splinters of wood and mountains of blood?
No, never; I denounce!
I denounce the conspiracy
of these deserted offices
that deny all agony,
that erase the design of the forest;
and I offer myself to be eaten by the stampeded cattle,
when their bellowing fills the valley

ALL: where the Hudson flows, drunk on oil.
(I, 517–19)

Ignacio Sánchez Mejías: "The man, the pure hero." As well as a *matador*, Sánchez Mejías was a poet, a playwright, and a close friend of Lorca's. Courtesy of Fundación Federico García Lorca.

LORCA: Spain is the only country where death is the national spectacle, where death sounds long trumpets at the arrival of springtime. (III, 317) The only serious thing left in the world is *toreo*. (Eisenberg 137) *Toreo* is the liturgy of the bulls, an authentic religious drama where, just as in the Mass, there is the adoration and sacrifice of a God.

In the bulls *duende* acquires its most moving effect because on one hand it has to struggle with death and on the other with geometry. The bull has one orbit; the *torero* has another. At the place where these lines intersect lies the point of danger of the terrible game. (III, 316)

Torero. Hero. Clock. Hero within a measure of time. Hero within the narrow confines of art.

Out of the last prodigious generation of *toreros* that Spain has given us, the place of faith belonged to

Ignacio Sanchez Mejías. Sánchez Mejías was faith, will, the man, the pure hero. (Eisenberg 137)

A las cinco de la tarde.
Eran las cinco en punto de la tarde.

¡Ay, que terribles cinco de la tarde!
¡Eran las cinco en todos los relojes!
¡Eran las cinco en sombra de la tarde!
(I, 551–52)

Ignacio Sanchez Mejías in the bullring of Cádiz less than a month before his fatal goring on August 11, 1934. Photo by Serrano. Courtesy of Fundacion Federico García Lorca.

Lament for Ignacio Sánchez Mejías

Goring and Death

v7 : At five in the afternoon.
It was exactly five in the afternoon.
A boy brought the white sheet
at five in the afternoon.
A basket of lime already prepared
at five in the afternoon.
The rest was death and only death
at five in the afternoon.

The wind blew away the cotton swabs
at five in the afternoon.
The dove and the leopard started to fight
at five in the afternoon.
And a thigh and a desolate horn
at five in the afternoon.
The bass chords began
at five in the afternoon.
Bells of arsenic and smoke
at five in the afternoon.
Groups in silence on the corners
at five in the afternoon.
And only the bull high-hearted!
At five in the afternoon.
When the icy sweat broke out
at five in the afternoon,
and iodine covered the ring
at five in the afternoon,
death laid her eggs in the wound
at five in the afternoon.
At five in the afternoon.
At exactly five in the afternoon.

The bed is a coffin on wheels
at five in the afternoon.
Flutes and bones throbbed in his ears
at five in the afternoon.
The bull bellowed in his head
at five in the afternoon.
The room shimmered with agony
at five in the afternoon.
Gangrene came from far away
at five in the afternoon.
The lily's horn through the green groin
at five in the afternoon.
The wounds burned like suns
at five in the afternoon,
and the crowd broke through the windows
at five in the afternoon.

At five in the afternoon.
Ay, that awful five in the afternoon!
It was five in the afternoon!
It was five on all the clocks!
It was five in the shadow of the afternoon!
(I, 551–52)

The Spilled Blood

ALL: I don't want to see it!

  v1: Tell the moon to come out.
     I don't want to see the blood
     of Ignacio running over the sand.

     I don't want to see it!

  v2: Full moon rising.
     Horse of quiet clouds.
     The bullring gray in dream
     with willows lining the stands.

     I don't want to see it!

  v3: My memory is on fire.
     Tell the jasmines to bring
     their blooms of tiny whiteness.

I don't want to see it!

v4: The cow of the ancient world
    licked her sad tongue
    over the muzzles of blood
    spilled in the sand,
    and the bulls of Guisando,
    almost death and almost stone,
    bellowed like two centuries
    weary of ranging the earth.
    No.
    I don't want to see it!

v5: Ignacio climbed the tiers
    with all his death on his back.
    He searched for the dawn
    and there was no dawn.
    He sought his strong profile
    and the dream misled him.
    He looked for his handsome body
    and found his running blood.
    Don't tell me to see it!

v7: I don't want to feel the spurt
    weaker with every beat;
    that spurt that lights up the stands
    and spills on the corduroy and leather
    of the thirsty crowds.
    Who shouts at me to come near?
    Don't tell me to see it!

v6: His eyes never shut
    when he saw the horns come close,
    but the terrible mothers
    lifted up their heads.
    And all across the bull ranches
    rose an air of secret voices
    calling to celestial bulls,
    to herdsmen of pale clouds.
    There was never a prince in Sevilla
    who could compare with him.
    No sword like his sword.
    No heart so true.
    Like a river of lions

his marvelous strength,
like a torso in marble
his finely chiseled wisdom.
An aura of Andalusian Rome
glowed around his head,
and his smile was a blossom
of intelligence and wit.
What a great *torero* in the ring!

v7: What a good mountain man in the *sierra!*

v1: How gentle with the spikes of wheat!

v2: How hard with the spurs!

v3: How tender with the dew!

v4: How dazzling at *fiesta!*

v5: How tremendous with the ultimate
banderillas of darkness!

v7: But now he sleeps without end.
Now the mosses and the grass
open with their sure fingers
the flower of his skull.
And his blood is already singing,
singing over marshes and meadows,
sliding past frozen horns,
stumbling on thousands of hooves,
like a long, dark, sad tongue
to form a pool of agony
by the Guadalquivir of the stars.

ALL: Oh, white wall of Spain!
Oh, black bull of pain!
Oh, hard blood of Ignacio!
Oh, nightingale of his veins!
No.
I don't want to see it!

v1: There is no chalice could hold it,

v2: no swallows could drink it,

v3: no glittering frost could cool it,

v5: no chant, no rain of lilies,

v6: no crystal could cover it in silver.

ALL: No.
I do not want to see it!
(I, 553–55)

from *Lying in State*

v4: There on the slab lies highborn Ignacio.
It's over. What happened? Look at his figure:
death has covered him in pale sulphur
and given him the head of a dark minotaur.

It's over. Rain falls in his mouth.
His last fleeting breath has sunken his chest,
and Love, soaked in tears of snow,
warms herself in the highland ranches.

What are they saying? A stinking silence falls.
This body which lies in state is fading away;
this firm figure once alive with nightingales
is filling with bottomless holes.

Who wrinkles the shroud? What they say is not true!
No one sings here, nor weeps in the corner,
no one pricks his spurs, nor startles a snake;
here I want only eyes wide open
to see this body with no possible rest.

Here I want to see men with hard voices,
men who break horses and tame rivers,
men whose bones crack and who sing
with a mouth full of sunlight and flint.

I want to see them here. In front of this slab.
In front of this body with broken reins.
I want them to show me the way out
for this captain bound by death.

I want them to show me a lament like a river
with sweet mists and deep banks
to bear Ignacio's body until it's lost
beyond the double snorting sound of bulls.

Lost in the round ring of the moon
that feigns when young a sad, motionless cow;
lost in the voiceless night of fishes,
lost in the white thickets of frozen smoke.

I don't want them to cover his face,
don't want him to get used to his death.
Go, Ignacio: Ignore the hot bellowing.
Sleep, fly, rest: Even the sea will die!
(I, 556–57)

Soul Departed

v 1 : The bull does not know you nor the fig tree,
nor the horses nor the ants of your house.
The boy does not know you nor the afternoon
because you have died forever.

v 3 : The slab of stone does not know you,
nor the black satin where you rot.
Your own mute memory does not know you
because you have died forever.

v 5 : Autumn will come with the shepherds' horns,
grapes in the mist and huddled mountains,
but no one will want to look into your eyes
because you have died forever.

v 6 : Because you have died forever,
like all the dead of the earth,
like all the dead that are forgotten
in a heap of snuffed-out dogs.

v 7 : No one knows you. No. But I sing of you.
I sing for tomorrow your profile and grace.
The signal maturity of your wisdom.
Your appetite for death and the taste of her mouth.
The sadness held in your valorous joy.

v 2 : It will be a long time
before an Andalusian so true, so rich in adventure,
is ever born again.
I sing your elegance with words that moan
and remember a sad wind in the olive trees.
(I, 558)

Federico García Lorca. *Busto de hombre muerte* [181]. Bust of dead man. © Visual 1992.

Federico García Lorca. *Rosa de la muerte. Caligrama* [291].
Rose of death. "Calligram."

LORCA: Life is laughter amid a rosary of death. (Cummings
178) Death. In each thing there is an insinuation of
death. Stillness, silence, serenity are all
apprenticeships. Death is everywhere, dominating. (III,
601) What matters most has an ultimate metallic
quality of death. The chasuble and the wagon wheel,
the razor and the prickly beards of shepherds, the bare
moon, a fly, humid cupboards, rubble piles, the images
of saints covered in lace, quicklime, and the wounding
edges of the rooflines and watchtowers—in Spain all
these things have minute grass-blades of death,
allusions and voices perceptible to an alert spirit that
bring to mind the dead air of our own passing. (III, 313)

from *The Shadow of My Soul*

v5 : The shadow of my soul
flees across a sunset of alphabets,
through a fog of books
and words.

The shadow of my soul!

The snowflake of pain
is melting,
but the reason and the substance
of my old noonday of lips,
of my old noonday
of looks,
remain.

A hallucination
milks my looks
and I see the word "love"
crumbling.

Nightingale of mine!
Nightingale!
Do you still sing?
(I, 32–33)

Federico García
Lorca. *Dos figuras
sobre una tumba*
[177]. Two figures
over a tomb.

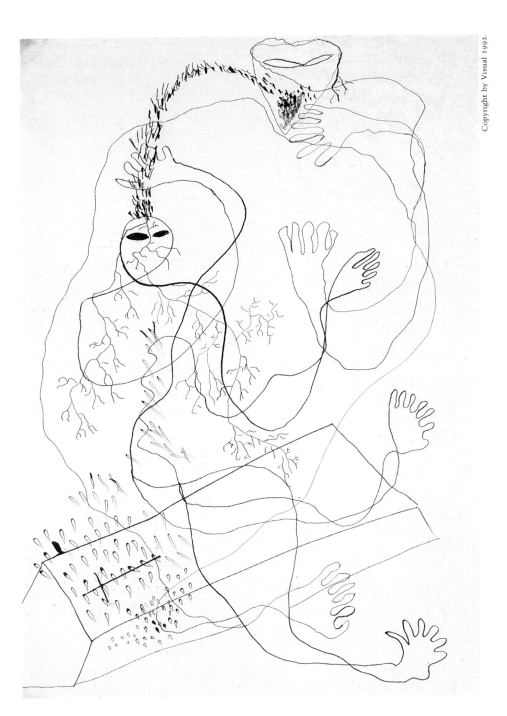

Omega

(poem for the dead)

v 6 : The weeds.
 I will cut off my right hand.
 Wait.
 The weeds.
 I have one glove of mercury, the other of silk.
 Wait.
 The weeds!
 Don't sob. Hush or they'll hear us.
 Wait.
 The weeds!
 The statues toppled over
 when the big door swung open.
 The weeds!!
 (I, 1061)

Federico García Lorca.
Rua da morte [292.5].
Street of death.

The Leave-Taking

v3 : If I die,
   leave the balcony open.

   The boy eats oranges.
   (From the balcony I see him.)

   The reaper cuts the wheat.
   (From my balcony I feel it.)

   If I die,
   leave the balcony open!
   (I, 364)

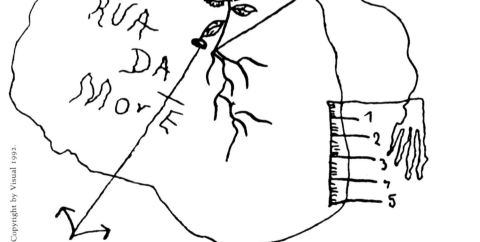

from *Amor de Don Perlimplín*

v 7 : Love, love
I lie here wounded.
So wounded by love's going;
so wounded,
dying of love.
Tell everyone that it was only
the nightingale.
A surgeon's knife with four sharp edges;
a bleeding throat and oblivion.
Take me by the hand, my love,
for I come quite badly wounded,
so wounded by love's going.
So wounded!
Dying of love!
(II, 479–80)

Memento

v 1 : When I die,
bury me with my guitar
beneath the sand.

When I die,
among the orange trees
and the sprigs of mint.

When I die,
bury me, if you like,
within a weather vane.

When I die!
(I, 208)

Federico García Lorca.
Guitarra [269]. Guitar.

from *Song of the Little Death*

v2 : Mortal meadow with moons
and blood beneath the earth.
Meadow of ancient blood.

I found myself with death.
Mortal meadow of earth.
A little death.

Cathedral of ash.
Light and night of sand.
A little death.

One death and I one man.
A man alone and she,
a little death.

One man. So what? What I said.
One man alone and she.
Meadow, love, light, and sand.
(I, 1062)

Federico García Lorca.
Marinero ahogado [292.2].
Drowned sailor.

Childhood and Death

v4: To find my childhood. My God! Empty pigeon coops.
I ate rotten oranges and old pieces of paper.
And I found my small body eaten by the rats,
at the bottom of the cistern, with the long lank hair of the
  insane.
My sailor suit
was soaked with no whale blubber,
but it showed the vulnerable eternity of photographs.
Drowned, yes, quite drowned. Sleep my little son, sleep.
A defeated child at school and in the waltz of the wounded
  rose,
frightened by the dark dawn of hair on his thighs,
agonizing with his own man who chewed tobacco down in
  his sinister side.
I hear a dry river full of tin fruit cans
where the sewers sing and they throw in shirts full of
  blood,
a river of rotten cats pretending to be corollas and
  anemones
to trick the moon into leaning on them sweetly.
Here alone with my drowned boy.
Here alone with a breeze of cold moss and tin can tops.
Here alone I see they have locked me out.
They have locked me out and there is a group of dead
  children
playing hit the bull's eye and another group of the dead
searching through the kitchen for melon rinds,
and one solitary, blue, inexplicably dead boy
searching for me along the stairways, reaching his hands
  into the cistern
while the stars fill the locks of the cathedrals with ashes
and all the people suddenly find themselves with their
  suits too short.
To find my childhood. My God!
I ate squashed lemons, stables, faded newspapers.
But my childhood was a rat fleeing through the darkest
  garden,
a rat with golden funeral ribbons clutched in his tiny
  teeth.
(I, 1048–49)

from *Fable and Round of the Three Friends*

LORCA: *Cuando se hundieron las formas puras*
bajo el cri cri de las margaritas,
comprendí que me habían asesinado.
Recorrieron los cafés y los cementerios y las iglesias,
abrieron los toneles y los armarios,
destrozaron tres esqueletos para arrancar sus dientes
    de oro.
Ya no me encontraron.
¿No me encontraron?
No. No me encontraron.
Pero se supo que la sexta luna huyó torrente arriba,
y que el mar recordó ¡de pronto!
los nombres de todos sus ahogados.

When the pure forms sunk
beneath the cries of the daisies,
I understood they had assassinated me.
They scoured the cafés, and the cemeteries, and the
    churches,
they opened the casks and the closets,
and destroyed three skeletons for their gold teeth.
But they never found me.
Never found me?
No. Never found me.
Yet it was known that the sixth moon fled up the
    torrent,
and the sea remembered at once
the names of all of her drowned.
(I, 451)

FINIS

114

Federico García Lorca. *Cabezas cortadas de Federico García Lorca y Pablo Neruda* [290.10]. Severed heads of Federico García Lorca and Pablo Neruda.

The following poems were translated for, but not included in, the final performance script of *Only Mystery*.

Landscape

The mistaken afternoon
wrapped herself in a chill.

Behind the dirty windowpanes
the children watch a yellow tree
turning into birds.

The afternoon is lying down
all along the river.
And a blush of apples
shivers on the rooftops.
(I, 303)

In Memoriam

(August 1920)

Sweet poplar,
sweet poplar,
you have turned
to gold.
Yesterday you were green,
a wild green
of glorious birds.
Today you are crestfallen

beneath the August sky
as I am beneath the red sky
of my spirit.
The captive fragrance
of your trunk
will come into my pious
heart.
Rude grandfather of the meadow!
We
have turned
to gold.
(I, 65)

Longing to Be a Statue

Sound.
Though nothing is left but the sound.

Scent.
Though nothing is left but the scent.

But tear away the memory
and the color of the old hours.

Grief.
Facing the magic and living grief.

Battle.
In the authentic and dirty battle.

But take away the invisible people
forever circling my house!
(I, 388)

Narcissus

Boy.
You're going to fall in the river!

> Deep below is a rose,
> in the rose another river.

Look at that bird!
Look at the yellow bird!

> My eyes have fallen
> deep beneath the water.

Oh, my God!
He's sliding in! *Muchacho!*

> . . . and I myself in the rose.

When he slipped beneath the water
I understood. But I cannot explain.
(I, 325–26)

Casida *of the Reclining Woman*

Seeing you naked is remembering the earth.
Flat earth, free of horses.
Earth without a reed, pure form
sealed to the future: horizon of silver.

Seeing you naked is feeling the yearning
of rain for the soft waist,
or the fever in the huge face of the sea
when no light shines on its cheek.

Blood will roar in the bedrooms
and come with a shining sword,
but you will not know where
the toad's heart or the violet are hiding.

Your womb is a tangle of roots,
your lips a shapeless dawn.
Beneath the warm roses of your bed
the dead moan awaiting their turn.
(I, 592)

Granada and 1850

From my room
I hear the fountain.

A finger of the grapevine
and a ray of sun
point at the place of my heart.

The clouds drift
through the August air. And I
dream that I do not dream
there within the fountain.
(I, 375)

Ballad of a Day in July

Silver bells
on the oxen.

"Where are you going,
maiden of sun and snow?"

"I go to the daisies
in the green meadow."

"The meadow is far away;
surely you're afraid."

"My love has no fear
of the wind nor of the shadows."

"You should fear the sun,
maiden of sun and snow."

"It's gone from my locks,
now and forevermore."

"Who are you, white child?
From whence do you come?"

"From stories of love
and from fountains come I."

Silver bells
on the oxen.

"What is that on your lips,
glowing like a fire?"

"It's the star of my lover
who lives and dies."

"What is that on your breast,
so sharp and light?"

"It's the sword of my lover
who lives and dies."

"What is that in your eyes,
so solemn and black?"

"My doleful thoughts
that always pain me so."

"Why do you wear a mantle
black like the color of death?"

"*Ay*, because I'm the widow,
now alone and bereaved

of the famous Count Laurel,
Laurel de los Laureles!"

"Then whom do you seek here,
if you're in love with no one else?"

"I seek the body of my Count,
Laurel de los Laureles."

"Could you be looking for love,
my deceitful, little widow?
I think you're looking for love,
and would to God you find it."

"The little stars in the heavens,
they're what I've been wanting.
Where will I find my lover,
who lives and dies?"

"He's dead beneath the water,
my little maiden of snow,
covered now in nostalgia
and carnations.

"*Ay*, knight-errant
of the cypress trees,

my soul would offer you
a lovely moonlit night."

"Ah, enraptured Isis!
maiden without adornment,
you tell your tale
through the mouths of children.
I offer you my tender heart,
wounded by the eyes of women."

"Gallant knight,
may God be with you.
I will go to search for my Count
Laurel de los Laureles."

"*Adiós*, my little maiden.
Sleeping rose,
you go on to love,
I go on to death."

Silver bells
on the oxen.

My heart bleeds
like a fountain.
(I, 62–64)

Pueblo

On the bare mountain
a calvary.
Clear water
and ancient olive trees.
In the winding streets
men in dark capes,
and atop the towers
weather vanes are turning.
Eternally
turning.
Oh, lost *pueblo*
in the Andalucía
of the lament!
(I, 168)

Death

What an effort!
The horse's effort to be a dog!
The dog's effort to be a swallow!
The swallow's effort to be a bee!
The bee's effort to be a horse!
And the horse,
what a sharp arrow it squeezes from the rose!
What a gray rose rises from its muzzle!
And the rose,
what a flock of howls and lights
it binds in the living sugar of its stem!
And sugar,
what little daggers it dreams in its vigils!
And the little daggers,
what a moon with no stables! What nudes,
eternal skin and blushes, they seek!
And I, in the gables,
what a seraph of flames I seek and am!
But a whitewashed archway,
how grand, how invisible, how tiny,
with no effort at all!
(I, 503)

Ballad of the Moon, the Moon

The moon came down to the forge
dressed in her bustle of nard.
The young boy stares and stares.
The boy is staring at the moon.
In the charged and sentient air
the moon raises her arms
and reveals, lubricious and pure,
her breasts of hard white tin.
Run away moon, moon, moon.
If the Gypsies come back,
they'll use your heart
for necklaces and rings of tin.

Niño, let me dance.
When the Gypsies get back,
they'll find you on that anvil
with your eyes closed tight.
Run away, moon, moon, moon.
I can hear their horses now.
Niño, let me be, don't step
on my starched white train.

A horseman was drawing near
beating the drum of the plain.
Within the forge
the boy has closed his eyes.
Across the olive grove
ride Gypsies of bronze and dream,
holding high their heads,
squinting with their eyes.

How the owl shrieks,
ay, how it shrieks from its tree!
Across the sky rides the moon
with a little boy by the hand.

Within the forge the Gypsies
weep, shouting out their grief.
The air veils and veils.
The air is veiling the moon.
(I, 393–94)

BIBLIOGRAPHY

Caro Baroja, Julio. *Los pueblos de España*. Madrid: Istmo, 1976.

Cummings, Philip. "The Mind of Genius." In *Songs*, written by Federico García Lorca and translated by Philip Cummings. Pittsburgh: Duquesne University Press, 1976.

De la Guardia, Alfredo. *García Lorca: Persona y creación*. Buenos Aires: Schapire, 1941.

Dominguín, Luis Miguel. "Introduction." In *Pablo Picasso: Toros y toreros*. New York: Harry N. Abrams, 1961.

Eisenberg, Daniel. "Un texto lorquiano descubierto en Nueva York: La presentación de Ignacio Sánchez Mejías." *Bulletin Hispanique* 80, nos. 1–2 (1978): 134–37.

García Lorca, Federico. *Obras completas*. Edited by Arturo del Hoyo. 3 vols. Madrid: Aguilar, 1986.

Hernández, Mario. *Libro de los dibujos de Federico García Lorca*. Madrid: Ediciones Tabapress/Fundación Federico García Lorca, 1990. In English: *Line of Light and Shadow: The Drawings of Federico García Lorca*. Translated by Christopher Maurer. Durham, N.C.: Duke University Press, 1991.

Josephs, Allen. *White Wall of Spain: The Mysteries of Andalusian Culture*. Ames, Iowa: Iowa State University Press, 1983. Reprinted with a new preface. Gainesville: University Presses of Florida/University of West Florida Press, 1990.

Maurer, Christopher. *Federico García Lorca escribe a su familia desde Nueva York y la Habana*. Madrid: Ministerio de Cultura, 1986.

Miró, Joan. In "Dibujos: Federico García Lorca," catalog for an exposition of Lorca's drawings, May 16–June 30, 1990, Casa de España, Paris.

Oppenheimer, Helen. *Lorca: The Drawings*. London: The Herbert Press, 1986.

Rodrigo, Antonina. *García Lorca en Cataluña*. Barcelona: Planeta, 1975.

Zukav, Gary. *The Dancing Wu Li Masters: An Overview of the New Physics*. New York: Bantam Books, 1980.

INDEX OF POEMS